contents

D1513453

roasted vegetable and balsamic salad

¼ cup (60ml) olive oil
1 clove garlic, crushed
2 large zucchini (300g)
4 medium flat mushrooms (500g), quartered
4 large egg tomatoes (360g), quartered
1 medium red onion (170g), cut into wedges
150g lamb's lettuce, trimmed
⅓ cup coarsely chopped fresh basil
dressing
¼ cup (60ml) olive oil
2 tablespoons balsamic vinegar
½ teaspoon sugar
½ teaspoon dijon mustard
1 clove garlic, crushed

Preheat oven to hot. Combine oil and garlic in small bowl.
Halve zucchini lengthways then chop into pieces on the diagonal.
Arrange vegetables, in single layer, on oven trays; brush with garlic-flavoured oil. Roast, uncovered, in hot oven about 20 minutes or until browned lightly and just tender. Remove vegetables from oven; cool.
Combine cold vegetables in large bowl with lettuce and basil. Add dressing; toss to combine.
Dressing Combine ingredients in screw-top jar; shake well.

serves 4
per serving 28.2g fat; 1321kJ (316 cal)

vietnamese prawn soup

12 uncooked medium king prawns (540g)
4cm piece fresh ginger (20g), sliced thinly
1 teaspoon black peppercorns
2 cloves garlic, crushed
2 fresh long red chillies, seeded, sliced thinly
1 stalk lemon grass, sliced coarsely
3 litres (12 cups) water
400g fresh rice noodles
¼ cup (60ml) lemon juice
⅓ cup (80ml) fish sauce, approximately
2 green onions, sliced thinly
⅓ cup firmly packed fresh coriander leaves
¼ cup firmly packed fresh mint leaves

Peel and devein prawns; discard heads. Place
prawn shells, ginger, peppercorns, garlic, half of the chilli,
lemon grass and the water in large saucepan. Bring to a boil,
reduce heat; simmer, uncovered, 20 minutes. Strain stock,
discard solids, then return liquid to clean saucepan.
Add prawns to stock; simmer, covered, until prawns
have changed colour.
Meanwhile, pour boiling water over rice noodles
in medium bowl; drain well.
Add lemon juice to stock; gradually add fish sauce to taste.
Divide prawns and noodles evenly among serving bowls;
top with stock, green onion, herbs and remaining chilli.

serves 6
per serving 1g fat; 756kJ (180 cal)

pork, chicken and rice noodle stir-fry

¼ cup (55g) sugar
⅓ cup (80ml) mild chilli sauce
¼ cup (60ml) fish sauce
1 tablespoon light soy sauce
1 tablespoon tomato sauce
500g chicken breast fillets, sliced thickly
150g fresh wide rice noodles
1 tablespoon sesame oil
500g pork mince
1 large brown onion (200g), sliced thickly
2 cloves garlic, crushed
2 cups (160g) bean sprouts
1 cup coarsely chopped fresh coriander
⅓ cup (50g) coarsely chopped roasted peanuts

Combine sugar and sauces in large bowl.
Add chicken; toss to coat in mixture.
Rinse noodles in strainer under hot water.
Separate noodles with fork; drain.
Meanwhile, drain chicken mixture; reserve marinade.
Heat half of the oil in wok or large frying pan; stir-fry
chicken mixture, in batches, until chicken is browned
all over and cooked through.
Heat remaining oil in wok; stir-fry pork, onion and garlic
until pork is cooked through. Return chicken to wok with
reserved marinade. Stir-fry until marinade comes to a boil;
remove from heat. Add noodles, sprouts, coriander and
peanuts; toss gently to combine.

serves 4
per serving 27.2g fat; 2707kJ (648 cal)

penne puttanesca

500g penne pasta
⅓ cup (80ml) extra virgin olive oil
3 cloves garlic, crushed
1 teaspoon dried chilli flakes
5 medium tomatoes (950g), chopped coarsely
1¼ cups (200g) seeded kalamata olives
8 anchovy fillets, drained, chopped coarsely
⅓ cup (65g) rinsed drained capers
⅓ cup coarsely chopped fresh flat-leaf parsley
2 tablespoons finely shredded fresh basil

Cook pasta in large saucepan of boiling water, uncovered, until just tender; drain.
Meanwhile, heat oil in large frying pan; cook garlic, stirring, until fragrant. Add chilli and tomato; cook, stirring, 5 minutes. Add remaining ingredients; cook, stirring occasionally, about 5 minutes or until sauce thickens slightly.
Add pasta to puttanesca sauce; toss gently to combine.

serves 4
per serving 21.2g fat; 2822kJ (674 cal)

pork and lemon grass stir-fry

Palm sugar, made from the distilled sap of the sugar palm, is also known as jaggery or gula jawa and is available from Asian specialty shops; use brown sugar if unavailable.

1 tablespoon peanut oil
2 tablespoons finely chopped lemon grass
2 fresh small red thai chillies, chopped finely
2cm piece fresh galangal (35g), chopped finely
2 cloves garlic, crushed
500g pork mince
1 tablespoon thai-style red curry paste
100g green beans, chopped coarsely
1½ tablespoons fish sauce
2 tablespoons lime juice
1 tablespoon grated palm sugar
1 small red onion (100g), sliced thinly
2 green onions, sliced thinly
¼ cup firmly packed fresh thai basil leaves
½ cup firmly packed fresh coriander leaves
¼ cup (75g) roasted peanuts, chopped coarsely
4 iceberg lettuce leaves

Heat oil in wok or large frying pan; cook lemon grass, chilli, galangal and garlic, stirring, until fragrant. Add pork; cook, stirring, until cooked through. Add curry paste; cook, stirring, until fragrant.

Add beans, fish sauce, juice and sugar to wok; cook, stirring, about 5 minutes or until beans are just tender. Remove from heat.

Add onions, basil, coriander and half of the peanuts to pork mixture; stir to combine.

Serve pork mixture in lettuce cups sprinkled with remaining peanuts.

serves 4
per serving 25.2g fat; 1638kJ (391 cal)

greek chicken salad

You need to purchase a large barbecued chicken, weighing approximately 900g, for this recipe.

375g small shell pasta
¼ cup coarsely chopped fresh oregano
½ cup (125ml) olive oil
¼ cup (60ml) lemon juice
3 cups (480g) shredded cooked chicken
1 medium red onion (170g), sliced thinly
500g cherry tomatoes, quartered
2 lebanese cucumbers (260g), chopped coarsely
1 large green capsicum (350g), chopped coarsely
1 cup (120g) seeded kalamata olives
280g jar marinated artichoke hearts, drained,
    chopped coarsely
200g fetta cheese, chopped coarsely

Cook pasta in large saucepan of boiling water, uncovered, until just tender; drain. Rinse under cold water; drain.
Meanwhile, place 2 tablespoons of the oregano, oil and juice in screw-top jar; shake well.
Place pasta in large bowl with chicken, onion, tomato, cucumber, capsicum, olives, artichoke, cheese and dressing; toss gently to combine. Top salad with remaining oregano.

serves 4
per serving 52.4g fat; 4226kJ (1009 cal)
tips You can use your favourite kind of pasta for this recipe.
Use the oil from the artichokes to make the dressing if you wish.

green chilli stew

Round steak, skirt steak and gravy beef are also suitable for this recipe.

2 tablespoons olive oil
1kg beef chuck steak, cut into 3cm cubes
1 large brown onion (200g), sliced thinly
2 cloves garlic, sliced thinly
2 teaspoons ground cumin
2 fresh long green chillies, seeded, sliced thinly
2 cups (500ml) beef stock
1 tablespoon tomato paste
3 large egg tomatoes (270g), chopped coarsely
500g tiny new potatoes, halved
4 small flour tortillas
¼ cup coarsely chopped fresh coriander

Preheat oven to moderate.
Heat half of the oil in large flameproof baking dish; cook beef, in batches, stirring, until browned all over.
Heat remaining oil in same dish; cook onion, garlic, cumin and chilli, stirring, until onion softens. Add stock and paste; bring to a boil, stirring. Return beef to dish; cook, covered, in moderate oven 45 minutes.
Add tomato and potato; cook, covered, in moderate oven 35 minutes. Uncover; cook 20 minutes.
Meanwhile, cut each tortilla into six wedges. Place, in single layer, on oven trays; toast, uncovered, in moderate oven about 8 minutes or until crisp.
Stir coriander into stew just before serving with tortilla crisps and, if desired, grilled cobs of corn.

serves 4
per serving 24.7g fat; 2740kJ (655 cal)
tip The tortilla crisps can be prepared up to two days ahead and kept in an airtight container.

crab salad

500g fresh crab meat
250g chinese cabbage, chopped finely
1 lebanese cucumber (130g), seeded, chopped coarsely
1 medium red onion (170g), halved, sliced thinly
6 green onions, cut into 4cm lengths
1 cup loosely packed fresh thai mint leaves
dressing
2 cloves garlic, crushed
2 tablespoons lime juice
2 tablespoons fish sauce
1 tablespoon brown sugar
2 fresh small red thai chillies, chopped finely

Drain crab in strainer; remove any shell and, if necessary, shred meat to desired texture.
Combine crab in large bowl with cabbage, cucumber, onions and mint; pour in dressing, toss to combine.
Dressing Combine ingredients in screw-top jar; shake well.

serves 4
per serving 1g fat; 529kJ (126 cal)

creamy pasta
with ham and peas

500g tortiglioni or rigatoni pasta
1 tablespoon olive oil
200g sliced leg ham, chopped coarsely
1 medium brown onion (150g), sliced thinly
1 clove garlic, crushed
300ml cream
1 cup (125g) frozen peas
¾ cup (60g) flaked parmesan cheese

Cook pasta in large saucepan of boiling
water, uncovered, until just tender. Reserve
¼ cup (60ml) of the cooking liquid; drain pasta
and return to pan.
Meanwhile, heat oil in large frying pan, add ham;
cook, stirring, until crisp. Remove from pan. Add
onion and garlic to same frying pan; cook, stirring,
until onion is soft.
Add cream, peas and reserved cooking liquid
to pan; bring to a boil. Reduce heat; simmer,
uncovered, until sauce has thickened slightly.
Add sauce, ham and half of the cheese to
pasta; toss gently to combine. Serve sprinkled
with remaining cheese and cracked black pepper,
if desired.

serves 4
per serving 41.5g fat; 3707kJ (885 cal)

crispy noodle cabbage salad

*Crunchy or fried noodles are available round or flat –
either can be used in this salad.*

3 cups (240g) finely shredded cabbage
3 cups (240g) finely shredded red cabbage
300g packet crunchy noodles
8 green onions, chopped finely
½ cup finely chopped fresh flat-leaf parsley
2 tablespoons sesame seeds, toasted
dressing
1 tablespoon sesame oil
1 tablespoon peanut oil
2 tablespoons white vinegar
2 tablespoons light soy sauce
½ cup (125ml) sweet chilli sauce

Place cabbages, noodles, onion, parsley
and seeds in large bowl.
Pour over dressing; toss to combine.
Dressing Combine ingredients in screw-top jar;
shake well.

serves 4
per serving 22.8g fat; 1464kJ (350 cal)
tips Make this salad just before serving or the
noodles will lose their crispness.
The dressing can be made ahead of time.

vegetable couscous

350g kumara
1 tablespoon olive oil
60g butter
4 baby eggplants (240g), sliced thinly
1 large brown onion (200g), sliced thinly
¼ teaspoon cayenne pepper
2 teaspoons ground cumin
2 teaspoons ground coriander
1½ cups (375ml) vegetable stock
2 cups (400g) couscous
2 teaspoons grated lemon rind
2 cups (500ml) boiling water
400g can chickpeas, rinsed, drained
2 tablespoons lemon juice
100g baby spinach leaves
¼ cup loosely packed fresh flat-leaf parsley

Chop peeled kumara into 1cm cubes. Heat oil
and half of the butter in large frying pan; cook
kumara with eggplant and onion, stirring, until
vegetables brown.

Add spices; cook about 2 minutes or until just
fragrant. Stir in stock; bring to a boil. Reduce heat;
simmer, uncovered, about 15 minutes or until
vegetables are just tender.

Meanwhile, combine couscous in large heatproof
bowl with half of the remaining butter, rind and the
water. Cover; stand about 5 minutes or until water is
absorbed, occasionally fluffing couscous with fork.

Add chickpeas and remaining butter to vegetable
mixture; cook, stirring, until butter melts. Stir in
couscous, juice, spinach and parsley.

serves 4
per serving 20.1g fat; 3246kJ (777 cal)

lamb and noodles with plum sauce

500g hokkien noodles
2 tablespoons peanut oil
700g lamb eye of loin, sliced thinly
1 large brown onion (200g), sliced thickly
2 medium carrots (240g), sliced thinly
1 clove garlic, crushed
2cm piece fresh ginger (10g), grated
150g snow peas, halved
½ cup (125ml) plum sauce
1 tablespoon soy sauce
¼ cup (60ml) chicken stock
1 teaspoon sesame oil
2 tablespoons sesame seeds, toasted

Rinse and separate noodles under hot running water; drain. Transfer to large bowl.
Heat half of the oil in wok or large frying pan; stir-fry lamb, in batches, until browned.
Heat remaining oil in wok; stir-fry onion until softened. Add carrot, garlic and ginger; stir-fry until vegetables are just tender.
Return lamb to wok with noodles, snow peas, combined sauces, stock and sesame oil; stir-fry until hot. Stir through toasted sesame seeds.

serves 4
per serving 26.6g fat; 2524kJ (603 cal)

coconut chicken masala

2 tablespoons peanut oil
1 large brown onion (200g), sliced thinly
2 cloves garlic, crushed
1 tablespoon coriander seeds
1 tablespoon ground cumin
1 teaspoon ground turmeric
1 teaspoon ground ginger
1 teaspoon garam masala
½ teaspoon ground cardamom
2 teaspoons chilli powder
1 teaspoon coarsely ground black pepper
1.5kg chicken breast fillets, chopped coarsely
¼ cup (70g) tomato paste
1½ cups (375ml) chicken stock
½ cup (125ml) water
1 teaspoon cornflour
¾ cup (180ml) coconut cream
2 tablespoons coarsely chopped fresh coriander

Heat oil in large saucepan; cook onion and garlic, stirring, until onion softens. Add coriander seeds; cook, stirring, about 1 minute or until seeds start to pop. Add remaining spices; cook, stirring, until mixture is fragrant.
Add chicken to pan, turning to coat pieces in spice mixture; cook, stirring, until chicken is just browned.
Stir in tomato paste, stock and the water; bring to a boil. Reduce heat; simmer, covered, about 20 minutes or until chicken is cooked through.
Blend cornflour with coconut cream in small bowl; stir into chicken curry. Bring to a boil; cook, stirring, until mixture boils and thickens slightly. Just before serving, stir in fresh coriander.

serves 4
per serving 40.4g fat; 3089kJ (739 cal)

spinach, bacon and pine nut pasta

4 bacon rashers (280g), sliced thinly
¼ cup (40g) pine nuts
2 cloves garlic, crushed
500g pappardelle pasta
200g baby spinach leaves
⅓ cup (25g) grated parmesan cheese
¼ cup (60ml) extra virgin olive oil
2 teaspoons lemon juice

Place bacon in small, non-stick frying pan; cook, stirring, until browned lightly. Add pine nuts and garlic; cook, stirring, until browned.

Meanwhile, cook pasta in large saucepan of boiling water, uncovered, until just tender. Reserve ¼ cup (60ml) of the cooking liquid, then drain pasta. Return pasta to saucepan.

Add spinach, cheese, bacon mixture, oil, juice and reserved cooking liquid to pasta; toss to combine. Sprinkle with extra parmesan cheese flakes, if desired.

serves 4
per serving 25.1g fat; 2847kJ (680 cal)

pork and prawn with crispy fried noodles

Palm sugar, made from the distilled sap of the sugar palm, is also known as jaggery or gula jawa and is available from Asian specialty shops; use brown sugar if unavailable.

300g fresh silken firm tofu
vegetable oil,
    for deep-frying
60g rice vermicelli
2 tablespoons peanut oil
2 eggs, beaten lightly
1 tablespoon water
2 cloves garlic, crushed
2 fresh small red thai
    chillies, chopped finely
1 fresh small green chilli,
    chopped finely
2 tablespoons grated
    palm sugar
2 tablespoons fish sauce
2 tablespoons
    tomato sauce
1 tablespoon rice
    wine vinegar
200g pork mince
200g small shelled
    cooked prawns,
    chopped coarsely
6 green onions, sliced thinly
¼ cup firmly packed fresh
    coriander leaves

Pat tofu all over with absorbent paper; cut into slices, then cut each slice into 1cm-wide matchsticks. Spread tofu on tray lined with absorbent paper; cover tofu with more absorbent paper, stand at least 10 minutes.

Meanwhile, heat vegetable oil in wok or large saucepan; deep-fry vermicelli quickly, in batches, until puffed. Drain on absorbent paper.

Using same heated oil, deep-fry drained tofu, in batches, until lightly browned. Drain on absorbent paper. Cool oil; remove from wok and reserve for another use.

Heat 2 teaspoons of the peanut oil in same cleaned wok; add half of the combined egg and water, swirl wok to make thin omelette. Cook, uncovered, until egg is just set. Remove from wok; roll omelette, cut into thin strips. Heat another 2 teaspoons of the peanut oil in same wok; repeat process with remaining egg mixture.

Combine garlic, chillies, sugar, sauces and vinegar in small bowl; pour half of the chilli mixture into small jug, reserve.

Combine pork in bowl with remaining half of the chilli mixture. Heat remaining peanut oil in same wok; stir-fry pork mixture about 5 minutes or until pork is cooked through. Add prawns; stir-fry 1 minute. Add tofu; stir-fry, tossing gently to combine.

Remove wok from heat; add reserved chilli mixture and half of the onion, toss to combine. Add vermicelli; toss gently to combine. Sprinkle with remaining onion, omelette strips and coriander.

serves 4
per serving 25.8g fat; 1770kJ (423 cal)

thai chicken salad

Palm sugar, made from the distilled sap of the sugar palm, is also known as jaggery or gula jawa and is available from Asian specialty shops; use brown sugar if unavailable. You need to purchase a large barbecued chicken, weighing approximately 900g, for this recipe.

350g yellow string beans, trimmed, halved
1 teaspoon finely grated lime rind
2 tablespoons lime juice
1 tablespoon grated palm sugar
1 clove garlic, crushed
1 tablespoon peanut oil
½ cup finely chopped fresh mint
2 teaspoons sweet chilli sauce
1 tablespoon fish sauce
3 cups (480g) shredded cooked chicken
1 cup coarsely chopped fresh coriander
250g cherry tomatoes, halved
1 fresh small red thai chilli, chopped finely

Boil, steam or microwave beans until almost tender. Rinse under cold water; drain.
Meanwhile, combine rind, juice, sugar, garlic, oil, mint and sauces in large bowl. Add beans, chicken, three-quarters of the coriander and tomato; toss gently to combine.
Top salad with remaining coriander and chilli just before serving.

serves 4
per serving 15.5g fat; 1318kJ (315 cal)
tip Chopped snake beans can be substituted for the yellow string beans, if preferred.

microwave prawn and pea risotto

600g large cooked prawns
20g butter
1 small leek (200g), sliced thinly
2 cloves garlic, crushed
8 saffron threads
2 cups (400g) arborio rice
2 cups (500ml) boiling water
1 cup (250ml) dry white wine
1½ cups (375ml) fish stock
1 cup (160g) frozen peas
2 tablespoons coarsely chopped fresh chives
¼ cup (60ml) lemon juice
30g butter, extra

Shell and devein prawns, leaving tails intact.
Place butter, leek, garlic and saffron in large
microwave-safe bowl; cook in microwave oven
on HIGH (100%), covered, about 2 minutes or until
leek softens. Stir in rice; cook on HIGH (100%),
covered, 1 minute. Add the water, wine and stock;
cook on HIGH (100%), covered, 15 minutes,
pausing to stir three times during cooking.
Add peas and prawns (reserve a few for garnish,
if desired); cook on HIGH (100%), covered,
3 minutes. Stir in chives, juice and extra butter.

serves 4
per serving 12.2g fat; 2574kJ (615 cal)

satay beef stir-fry with hokkien noodles

600g hokkien noodles
300g beef rump steak, sliced thinly
1cm piece fresh ginger (5g), grated
2 teaspoons sesame oil
1 small red onion (100g), sliced thinly
1 medium red capsicum (200g), sliced thinly
150g broccoli florets
2 teaspoons lime juice
¼ cup (60ml) satay sauce
1 tablespoon hoisin sauce
⅓ cup (80ml) soy sauce
1 tablespoon kecap manis
150g snow peas
1 tablespoon finely chopped fresh coriander
¼ cup (35g) unsalted roasted peanuts,
    chopped coarsely

Rinse noodles under hot water; drain. Transfer
to large bowl; separate noodles with fork.
Heat oiled wok or large non-stick frying pan; stir-fry
beef and ginger, in batches, until browned.
Heat oil in wok; stir-fry onion, capsicum and broccoli
until just tender. Return beef to wok with combined
juice and sauces; stir-fry until sauce boils. Add
noodles and snow peas; stir-fry until hot.
Add coriander; stir-fry until combined. Serve
sprinkled with nuts.

serves 4
per serving 15.6g fat; 1800kJ (430 cal)

chickpea, pumpkin and eggplant curry

1 tablespoon vegetable oil
1 medium brown onion (150g), chopped coarsely
2 cloves garlic, crushed
4 baby eggplants (200g), chopped coarsely
¼ cup (75g) medium curry paste
½ cup (600g) butternut pumpkin, peeled,
    chopped coarsely
½ cauliflower (500g), chopped
1½ cups (375ml) vegetable stock
425g can crushed tomatoes
400g can chickpeas, rinsed, drained
1 cup (280g) yogurt
½ cup finely shredded fresh mint

Heat oil in large saucepan, add onion, garlic
and eggplant; cook, stirring, until just tender.
Add curry paste; cook, stirring, until fragrant.
Add pumpkin, cauliflower, stock and undrained
tomatoes, bring to a boil; simmer, covered,
20 minutes. Add chickpeas; simmer, covered,
10 minutes or until vegetables are tender.
Meanwhile, combine yogurt and mint in
small bowl.
Serve curry with yogurt mixture.

serves 4
per serving 15g fat; 1389kJ (332 cal)

tom kha gai

This Thai chicken soup is one of our favourites. You need to purchase a large barbecued chicken, weighing approximately 900g, for this recipe.

2 teaspoons peanut oil
1 tablespoon finely chopped lemon grass
3cm piece fresh ginger (15g), grated
1 clove garlic, crushed
3 fresh small green chillies, chopped finely
4 kaffir lime leaves, sliced thinly
¼ teaspoon ground turmeric
3¼ cups (800ml) light coconut milk
3 cups (750ml) chicken stock
2 cups (500ml) water
1 tablespoon fish sauce
3 cups (480g) shredded cooked chicken
3 green onions, sliced thinly
¼ cup (60ml) lime juice
2 tablespoons coarsely chopped fresh coriander
⅓ cup (25g) bean sprouts
¼ cup loosely packed fresh mint leaves

Heat oil in large saucepan; cook lemon grass, ginger, garlic, chilli, lime leaves and turmeric, stirring, about 2 minutes or until fragrant.
Stir in coconut milk, stock, the water and sauce; bring to a boil. Add chicken, reduce heat; simmer, uncovered, 10 minutes.
Just before serving, stir in onion, juice and coriander. Serve topped with sprouts and mint.

serves 4
per serving 25.1g fat; 1648kJ (394 cal)

beef, red wine and chilli casserole with polenta

1 tablespoon olive oil
1.5kg beef chuck steak, cut into 3cm pieces
2 cloves garlic, crushed
3 fresh small red thai chillies, seeded, sliced thinly
2 teaspoons dijon mustard
1 large brown onion (200g), sliced thickly
2 medium tomatoes (380g), chopped coarsely
410g can tomato puree
¾ cup (180ml) dry red wine
½ cup (125ml) beef stock
1.125 litres (4½ cups) water
1 cup (170g) polenta
¼ cup (20g) finely grated parmesan cheese
2 tablespoons coarsely shredded fresh flat-leaf parsley

Heat oil in large saucepan; cook beef, in batches, until browned all over. Cook garlic, chilli, mustard and onion in same pan, stirring, until onion softens. Return beef to pan with tomato; cook, stirring, 2 minutes.
Add puree, wine, stock and ½ cup of the water to pan; bring to a boil. Reduce heat; simmer, covered, about 1½ hours or until beef is tender, stirring occasionally.
Meanwhile, bring the remaining water to a boil in medium saucepan. Gradually add polenta; cook, stirring, over medium heat about 10 minutes or until thickened. Stir cheese into polenta.
Sprinkle parsley over beef casserole just before serving with polenta.

serves 4
per serving 18.2g fat; 2934kJ (701 cal)

beef and rice noodle stir-fry

500g fresh rice noodles
2 tablespoons peanut oil
500g beef fillets, sliced thinly
1 clove garlic, crushed
4cm piece fresh ginger (20g), grated
1 tablespoon finely chopped lemon grass
1 fresh small red thai chilli, seeded, chopped finely
1 tablespoon coarsely chopped fresh mint
1 large carrot (180g), halved lengthways, sliced thinly
200g fresh baby corn, halved lengthways
200g chinese broccoli, chopped coarsely
1 tablespoon brown sugar
2 teaspoons cornflour
¼ cup (60ml) chinese cooking wine
¼ cup (60ml) oyster sauce
2 tablespoons light soy sauce

Rinse noodles under hot water; drain. Transfer to
large bowl; separate noodles with fork.
Heat half of the oil in wok or large frying pan; stir-fry beef,
in batches, until browned all over.
Heat remaining oil in wok; stir-fry garlic, ginger, lemon grass,
chilli and mint until fragrant. Add carrot and corn; stir-fry until
carrot is just tender.
Return beef to wok with broccoli, sugar and blended cornflour,
wine and sauces; stir-fry until broccoli just wilts, and sauce boils
and thickens slightly. Add noodles; stir-fry until hot.

serves 4
per serving 16.5g fat; 2011kJ (481 cal)
tip Fresh rice noodles must be rinsed under hot water to
remove starch and excess oil before using. You can substitute
egg noodles for the rice noodles, if you prefer.

lamb and spinach curry

This recipe, called saag gosht in India, is one of our favourites. You can use fresh spinach leaves if you like, but they need to be softened in boiling water then processed before using.

2 tablespoons vegetable oil
750g lamb fillets, sliced thinly
2 medium brown onions (300g),
    chopped finely
3 cloves garlic, crushed
2cm piece fresh
    ginger (10g), grated
1 teaspoon chilli powder
1 cinnamon stick
5 cloves
5 cardamom pods, bruised
2 teaspoons ground coriander
2 teaspoons ground cumin
½ teaspoon ground turmeric
1 tablespoon garam masala
2 teaspoons black
    mustard seeds
2 tablespoons tomato paste
600ml buttermilk
½ cup (120g) sour cream
600g frozen spinach,
    thawed, drained

Heat half of the oil in large saucepan; cook lamb, in batches, until browned all over.

Heat remaining oil in same pan; cook onion, garlic and ginger, stirring, until onion softens. Add spices and paste; cook, stirring, until fragrant.

Return lamb to pan with remaining ingredients; bring to a boil. Reduce heat; simmer, uncovered, about 15 minutes or until sauce thickens.

serves 4
per serving 32.6g fat; 2417kJ (578 cal)
tip Use your hands to squeeze out as much excess water from the spinach as possible.
serving suggestion Serve with steamed basmati rice and warm naan.

ginger beef stir-fry

Palm sugar, made from the distilled sap of the sugar palm, is also known as jaggery or gula jawa and is available from Asian specialty shops; use brown sugar if unavailable.

6cm piece fresh ginger (30g)
2 tablespoons peanut oil
600g beef rump steak, sliced thinly
2 cloves garlic, crushed
120g snake beans, cut into 5cm lengths
8 green onions, sliced thinly
2 teaspoons grated palm sugar
2 teaspoons oyster sauce
1 tablespoon fish sauce
1 tablespoon soy sauce
½ cup loosely packed fresh thai basil leaves

Slice peeled ginger thinly; stack slices, then slice again into thin slivers.
Heat half of the oil in wok; stir-fry beef, in batches, until browned all over.
Heat remaining oil in wok; stir-fry ginger and garlic until fragrant. Add beans; stir-fry until just tender.
Return beef to wok with onion, sugar and sauces; stir-fry until sugar dissolves and beef is cooked as desired. Remove from heat, toss basil leaves through stir-fry.

serves 4
per serving 19.8g fat; 1536kJ (367 cal)

rag pasta with pumpkin and sage

500g lasagne sheets
50g butter
¼ cup (60ml) extra virgin olive oil
1kg butternut pumpkin, sliced thinly
2 cloves garlic, sliced thinly
1 teaspoon fresh thyme leaves
½ cup (40g) grated parmesan cheese
2 teaspoons fresh sage leaves

Break lasagne sheets into large pieces.
Cook lasagne in large saucepan of boiling water
until just tender. Drain, reserving 2 tablespoons
of the cooking liquid.
Meanwhile, heat butter and oil in large non-stick
frying pan, add pumpkin; cook, stirring gently,
until pumpkin is just tender. Add garlic and thyme;
cook, stirring, until fragrant.
Add cheese and sage; gently toss pumpkin
mixture through pasta with the reserved cooking
liquid. Sprinkle with extra parmesan cheese
flakes, if desired.

serves 4
per serving 29.7g fat; 3175kJ (758 cal)

beef pho

Large bowls of pho are a breakfast favourite throughout Vietnam, but we like to eat it any time of day. Round, skirt or chuck steak are all suitable for this recipe. Gravy beef is also known as shin.

3 litres (12 cups) water
1kg gravy beef
1 star anise
2.5cm piece fresh galangal (45g)
¼ cup (60ml) soy sauce
250g bean thread noodles
1¼ cups (100g) bean sprouts
¼ cup loosely packed fresh coriander leaves
⅓ cup loosely packed fresh vietnamese mint leaves
4 green onions, sliced thinly
1 fresh long red chilli, sliced thinly
⅓ cup (80ml) lime juice

Combine the water, beef, star anise, galangal and soy sauce in large saucepan; bring to a boil. Reduce heat; simmer, covered, 30 minutes. Uncover; simmer 30 minutes or until beef is tender.

Meanwhile, place noodles in medium heatproof bowl, cover with boiling water; stand until just tender, drain. Rinse under cold water; drain.

Combine remaining ingredients in medium bowl.

Remove beef from pan; reserve broth in pan. Remove fat and sinew from beef, slice thinly. Return beef to pan; reheat until broth just comes to a boil.

Divide noodles among serving bowls; top with hot beef and broth then sprout mixture.

serves 6
per serving 7.6g fat; 1351kJ (323 cal)

fettuccine with rocket pesto and fresh tomato salsa

500g fettuccine pasta
8 cloves garlic, quartered
½ cup coarsely chopped fresh basil
120g rocket, chopped coarsely
⅔ cup (160ml) olive oil
½ cup (40g) finely grated parmesan cheese
3 medium tomatoes (570g), chopped coarsely
2 tablespoons lemon juice
2 fresh small red thai chillies, sliced thinly
⅓ cup (50g) pine nuts, toasted

Cook pasta in large saucepan of boiling water, uncovered, until just tender; drain.
Meanwhile, blend or process garlic, basil, rocket and oil until smooth.
Combine pasta, rocket pesto, cheese, tomato, juice and chilli in large saucepan; cook, stirring, until hot. Add nuts; toss gently to combine.

serves 4
per serving 50.3g fat; 3780kJ (904 cal)
tip You could substitute baby spinach leaves for the rocket for a milder pesto.

balti biryani

This delectable Indian recipe combines rice and meat with a heady
mixture of aromatic spices. Biryanis are traditionally saved for special
occasions, but this version is simple enough to prepare at any time.
Round steak, chuck steak or gravy beef are also suitable for this recipe.

750g beef skirt steak,
cut into 2cm cubes
¾ cup (225g) balti
curry paste
2 cups (400g) basmati rice
8 cloves garlic, unpeeled
20g ghee
4 cardamom pods, bruised
4 cloves
1 cinnamon stick
3 green onions, sliced thinly
2 cups (500ml) beef stock
¾ cup (100g) toasted
slivered almonds
¼ cup loosely packed fresh
coriander leaves
2 fresh small red thai
chillies, sliced thinly

Preheat oven to moderate.

Combine beef and curry paste in medium
bowl, cover; refrigerate 1 hour.

Meanwhile, place rice in medium bowl,
cover with water; stand 30 minutes. Drain rice
in strainer; rinse under cold water, drain.

Meanwhile, place garlic in small baking dish;
roast, uncovered, in moderate oven about
20 minutes or until softened.

Melt ghee in large saucepan; cook cardamom,
cloves, cinnamon and onion, stirring, until
fragrant. Add beef mixture, reduce heat;
simmer, covered, stirring occasionally, about
45 minutes or until beef is tender.

Add rice with stock to pan; simmer, covered,
stirring occasionally, about 15 minutes or until
rice is just tender.

Peel garlic; chop finely. Add garlic, almonds
and coriander to biryani, cover; stand 5 minutes.
Sprinkle biryani with chilli; serve with raita
and naan, if desired.

serves 4
per serving 41.9g fat; 4016kJ (959 cal)

chicken and thai basil fried rice

You will need to cook about 1 ⅓ cups (265g) rice for this recipe.

¼ cup (60ml) peanut oil
1 medium brown onion (150g), chopped finely
3 cloves garlic, crushed
2 fresh long green chillies, seeded, chopped finely
1 tablespoon brown sugar
500g chicken breast fillets, chopped coarsely
2 medium red capsicums (400g), sliced thinly
200g green beans, chopped coarsely
4 cups cooked jasmine rice
2 tablespoons fish sauce
2 tablespoons soy sauce
½ cup loosely packed fresh thai basil leaves

Heat oil in wok or large frying pan; stir-fry onion, garlic and chilli until onion softens. Add sugar; stir-fry until dissolved. Add chicken; stir-fry until lightly browned. Add capsicum and beans; stir-fry until vegetables are just tender and chicken is cooked through.
Add rice and sauces; stir-fry, tossing gently to combine. Remove from heat; add basil leaves, toss gently to combine.

serves 4
per serving 21.7g fat; 1922kJ (459 cal)

glossary

almonds, slivered small, lengthways-cut almonds.

arborio rice small, round-grained, absorbent white rice.

artichoke hearts tender centre of the globe artichoke; use fresh or purchase, in brine or oil, from supermarkets.

bacon rasher also known as bacon slices; made from cured and smoked pork side.

basil
thai: also known as horapa, it has a slight licorice taste.
sweet: used extensively in Italian dishes.

basmati rice long-grained white rice; wash before using.

bean sprouts also known as bean shoots; tender growths of assorted beans and seeds.

bean thread noodles also known as cellophane or glass noodles; very fine noodles made from mung bean paste. Soak noodles to soften before use, unless deep-frying.

black mustard seeds also known as brown mustard seeds; used in most mustards.

butter use salted or unsalted (sweet) butter; 125g is equal to one stick of butter.

buttermilk sold in refrigerated dairy section in supermarkets. Made similarly to yogurt.

capers grey-green buds of a warm-climate shrub, sold dried and salted or pickled in a vinegar brine.

capsicum also known as bell pepper or, simply, pepper.

cardamom sweet, distinctive, aromatic spice available in pod, seed or ground form.

cayenne pepper very hot, dried red chilli; sold ground.

chickpeas also known as garbanzos, hummus or channa; round, beige-coloured legume.

chilli use rubber gloves when seeding and chopping fresh chillies as they can burn skin. Removing membranes and seeds lessens the heat level.
dried flakes: dehydrated fine slices and whole seeds.
thai: small, medium-hot, and bright red in colour.
powder: made from dried ground thai chillies; substitute for fresh chillies in proportion of ½ teaspoon ground chilli powder to 1 medium fresh chilli.
sweet chilli sauce: mild Thai sauce made from red chillies, sugar, garlic and vinegar.

chinese broccoli also known as gai lam, gai lum, chinese broccoli and chinese kale.

chinese cabbage also known as peking or napa cabbage, wong bok or petsai. Elongated in shape with crinkly leaves.

chinese cooking wine made from rice, wheat, sugar and salt, with 13.5% alcohol; buy from Asian food stores. Mirin or sherry can be substituted.

coconut cream obtained from first pressing of coconut flesh; available in cans and cartons.

coconut milk pure, unsweetened coconut milk; available in cans and cartons.

coriander also known as pak chee, cilantro or chinese parsley; leafy green herb.

cornflour also known as cornstarch; used as a thickening agent in cooking.

couscous a fine, grain-like cereal product, made from semolina.

crunchy noodles also known as fried or crispy noodles.

cumin also known as zeera.

dijon mustard pale brown, fairly mild French mustard.

eggplant also known as aubergine.

fetta cheese a crumbly goat- or sheep-milk cheese with a sharp, salty taste.

fish sauce also known as nam pla or nuoc nam. Made from salted, fermented fish.

galangal also known as ka; a root with a hot citrusy-ginger flavour. Available fresh and in a dried powder called laos.

garam masala roasted, ground spice blend; includes cardamom, cinnamon, cloves, coriander, fennel and cumin.

ghee clarified butter (the milk solids have been removed).

ginger also known as green or root ginger.

hoisin sauce sweet and spicy Chinese paste made from soy beans, onions and garlic.

hokkien noodles also known as stir-fry noodles; fresh wheat noodles needing no pre-cooking before use.

jasmine rice aromatic, long-grained white rice.

kaffir lime leaves also known as bai magrood; glossy dark green leaves joined end to end (in pairs). Used fresh or dried like bay or curry leaves.

kecap manis a dark, thick, sweet soy sauce.

kumara Polynesian name of orange-fleshed sweet potato.

lamb's lettuce also known as mâche, corn salad or lamb's tongue; tender, narrow, dark-green leaves with mild flavour.

lemon grass a tall, clumping, lemon-smelling and -tasting, sharp-edged grass; the white lower part of the stem is used.

mince also known as ground meat.

onion

green: also known as scallion or (incorrectly) shallot; immature onion picked before the bulb has formed, having a long, bright-green edible stalk.

red: also known as spanish, red spanish or bermuda onion; sweet purple-red onion.

oyster sauce rich sauce made from oysters and their brine, salt and soy sauce.

parsley, flat-leaf also known as continental or italian parsley.

pine nuts also known as pignoli; small kernels from cones of some pine trees.

polenta also known as cornmeal; flour-like cereal made from dried corn (maize). Also the name of the dish made from it.

prawns also known as shrimp.

pumpkin, butternut also known as butternut squash.

rice noodles, fresh can be purchased in various widths or large sheets; chewy and pure white, they do not need pre-cooking before use.

rice vermicelli similar to bean thread noodles, only longer and made with rice flour instead of mung bean starch.

rocket also known as arugula, rugula and rucola; a peppery-tasting green leaf.

saffron threads stigma of a member of the crocus family, available in strands or ground form; imparts a yellow-orange colour to food once infused.

satay sauce Indonesian or Malaysian spicy peanut sauce. Available in supermarkets.

sesame oil made from roasted, crushed white sesame seeds; used as a flavouring rather than as a cooking medium.

snake beans thin, long (about 40cm) fresh green beans.

snow pea also called mange tout ("eat all").

sour cream commercially cultured, thick soured cream; minimum fat content is 35%.

soy sauce also known as sieu; made from fermented soy beans. Several variations are available in most stores.

spinach also known as english spinach and, incorrectly, silverbeet. Tender green leaves are good raw or cooked.

star anise dried, star-shaped pod having an astringent aniseed flavour.

stock cubes or powder can be used. As a guide, 1 teaspoon of stock powder or 1 small crumbled stock cube mixed with 1 cup (250ml) water will give a fairly strong stock.

string beans, yellow also known as wax, french, butter and runner beans; yellow-coloured fresh "green" beans.

sugar we used coarse, granulated table sugar, also known as crystal sugar, unless otherwise specified.

brown: a soft, fine, granulated sugar retaining molasses to give its colour and flavour.

palm: also known as jaggery and jawa or gula melaka; made from the sap of sugar palm tree. Usually sold in rock-hard cakes; substitute with brown sugar.

thai mint also known as marsh mint; similar to spearmint. Has thick round leaves.

tofu also known as bean curd; off-white, custard-like product made from "milk" of crushed soy beans. Silken tofu refers to method of straining the soy bean liquid through silk.

tomato

cherry: also known as tiny tim or tom thumb tomatoes.

egg: also called plum or roma; smallish and oval-shaped.

paste: triple-concentrated tomato puree.

puree: canned pureed tomatoes (not tomato paste).

sauce: also known as catsup or ketchup; condiment made from tomato, vinegar and spice.

tortillas, flour thin, round unleavened bread; sold fresh, frozen or vacuum-packed.

vietnamese mint not really a mint, but a pungent, peppery narrow-leafed member of the buckwheat family. Also known as cambodian mint, laksa leaf and rau ram in Vietnam!

vinegar

balsamic: originally from Modena, Italy, there are now many balsamic vinegars on the market ranging in pungency and quality depending on the method and length of aging. Quality can be determined up to a point by price; use the most expensive sparingly.

rice wine: made from fermented rice, with no additives.

white: made from the spirit of cane sugar.

zucchini also known as courgette.

index

facts & figures

These conversions are approximate only, but the difference between an exact and the approximate conversion of various liquid and dry measures is minimal and will not affect your cooking results.

Measuring equipment
The difference between one country's measuring cups and another's is, at most, within a 2 or 3 teaspoon variance. (For the record, 1 Australian metric measuring cup holds approximately 250ml.) The most accurate way of measuring dry ingredients is to weigh them. For liquids, use a clear glass or plastic jug having metric markings.

Note: NZ, Canada, US and UK all use 15ml tablespoons. Australian tablespoons measure 20ml. All cup and spoon measurements are level.

How to measure
When using graduated measuring cups, shake dry ingredients loosely into the appropriate cup. Do not tap the cup on a bench or tightly pack the ingredients unless directed to do so. Level the top of measuring cups and measuring spoons with a knife. When measuring liquids, place a clear glass or plastic jug having metric markings on a flat surface to check accuracy at eye level.

Dry measures

metric	imperial
15g	½oz
30g	1oz
60g	2oz
90g	3oz
125g	4oz (¼lb)
155g	5oz
185g	6oz
220g	7oz
250g	8oz (½lb)
280g	9oz
315g	10oz
345g	11oz
375g	12oz (¾lb)
410g	13oz
440g	14oz
470g	15oz
500g	16oz (1lb)
750g	24oz (1½lb)
1kg	32oz (2lb)

We use large eggs with an average weight of 60g.

Liquid measures

metric	imperial
30 ml	1 fluid oz
60 ml	2 fluid oz
100 ml	3 fluid oz
125 ml	4 fluid oz
150 ml	5 fluid oz (¼ pint/1 gill)
190 ml	6 fluid oz
250 ml (1 cup)	8 fluid oz
300 ml	10 fluid oz (½ pint)
500 ml	16 fluid oz
600 ml	20 fluid oz (1 pint)
1000 ml (1 litre)	1¾ pints

Helpful measures

metric	imperial
3mm	⅛in
6mm	¼in
1cm	½in
2cm	¾in
2.5cm	1in
6cm	2½in
8cm	3in
20cm	8in
23cm	9in
25cm	10in
30cm	12in (1ft)

Oven temperatures
These oven temperatures are only a guide. Always check the manufacturer's manual.

	°C (Celsius)	°F (Fahrenheit)	Gas Mark
Very slow	120	250	½
Slow	140 – 150	275 – 300	1 – 2
Moderately slow	170	325	3
Moderate	180 – 190	350 – 375	4 – 5
Moderately hot	200	400	6
Hot	220 – 230	425 – 450	7 – 8
Very hot	240	475	9

at your fingertips

These elegant slipcovers store up to 10 mini books and make the books instantly accessible.

And the metric measuring cups and spoons make following our recipes a piece of cake.

Book Holder
Australia and overseas:
$8.95 (incl. GST).

Metric Measuring Set
Australia: $6.50 (incl. GST).
New Zealand: $A8.00.
Elsewhere: $A9.95.
Prices include postage and handling. This offer is available in all countries.

Mail or fax Photocopy and complete the coupon below and post to ACP Books Reader Offer, ACP Publishing, GPO Box 4967, Sydney NSW 2001, or fax to (02) 9267 4967.

Phone Have your credit card details ready, then phone 136 116 (Mon-Fri, 8.00am-6.00pm; Sat, 8.00am-6.00pm).

Australian residents We accept the credit cards listed on the coupon, money orders and cheques.

Overseas residents We accept the credit cards listed on the coupon, drafts in $A drawn on an Australian bank, and also UK, NZ and US cheques in the currency of the country of issue. Credit card charges are at the exchange rate current at the time of payment.

Photocopy and complete coupon below

☐ Book Holder   ☐ Metric Measuring Set

Please indicate number(s) required.

Mr/Mrs/Ms _____

Address _____

_____

Postcode _____ Country _____

Ph: Business hours ( ) _____

I enclose my cheque/money order for $ _____ payable to ACP Publishing.

OR: please charge $ _____ to my ☐ Bankcard ☐ Mastercard

☐ Visa ☐ American Express ☐ Diners Club

Expiry date ____ /____

Card number

Cardholder's signature _____

Please allow up to 30 days delivery within Australia.
Allow up to 6 weeks for overseas deliveries.
Both offers expire 31/12/05. HLMBF05

Food director Pamela Clark
Food editor Louise Patniotis
Nutritional information Laila Ibram

ACP BOOKS
Editorial director Susan Tomnay
Creative director Hieu Chi Nguyen
Senior editor Julie Collard
Designer Mary Keep
Studio manager Caryl Wiggins
Sales director Brian Cearnes
Publishing manager (rights & new projects) Jane Hazell
Brand manager Renée Crea
Sales & marketing coordinator Gabrielle Botto
Pre-press Harry Palmer
Production manager Carol Currie
Chief executive officer John Alexander
Group publisher Pat Ingram
Publisher Sue Wannan
Editor-in-chief Deborah Thomas
Produced by ACP Books, Sydney.
Printing by Dai Nippon Printing in Korea.
Published by ACP Publishing Pty Limited, 54 Park St, Sydney; GPO Box 4088, Sydney, NSW 2001.
Ph: (02) 9282 8618 Fax: (02) 9267 9438.
www.acpbooks.com.au
To order books phone 136 116.
Send recipe enquiries to Recipeenquiries@acp.com.au
Australia Distributed by Network Services, GPO Box 4088, Sydney, NSW 2001.
Ph: (02) 9282 8777 Fax: (02) 9264 3278.
United Kingdom Distributed by Australian Consolidated Press (UK), Moulton Park Business Centre, Red House Road, Moulton Park, Northampton, NN3 6AQ. Ph: (01604) 497 531 Fax: (01604) 497 533 acpukltd@aol.com
Canada Distributed by Whitecap Books Ltd, 351 Lynn Ave, North Vancouver, BC, V7J 2C4, Ph: (604) 980 9852 Fax: (604) 980 8197 customerservice@whitecap.ca
www.whitecap.ca
New Zealand Distributed by Netlink Distribution Company, ACP Media Centre, Cnr Fanshawe and Beaumont Streets, Westhaven, Auckland; PO Box 47906, Ponsonby, Auckland, NZ.
Ph: (09) 366 9966 ask@ndcnz.co.nz
South Africa Distributed by PSD Promotions, 30 Diesel Road, Isando, Gauteng, Johannesburg; PO Box 1175, Isando, 1600, Gauteng, Johannesburg.
Ph: (27 11) 392 6065/7 Fax: (27 11) 392 6079/80
orders@psdprom.co.za

Clark, Pamela.
The Australian Women's Weekly
Bowl Food.
Includes index.
ISBN 1 86396 363 4

1. Quick and easy cookery. 2. Cookery.
I. Title: Australian Women's Weekly.
641.5

© ACP Publishing Pty Limited 2004
ABN 18 053 273 546
This publication is copyright. No part of it may be reproduced or transmitted in any form without the written permission of the publishers.
First published 2004. Reprinted 2004, 2005.
Cover Rag pasta with pumpkin and sage, page 50 (photo by Brett Stevens, styling by Marie-Helene Clauzon).
Back cover at left, Lamb and spinach curry, page 46; at right, Crab salad, page 17.
Additional photography Brett Stevens
Additional styling Julz Beresford
Home economists Nancy Duran, Susan Riggall